I0157445

# Purrfect Poetry

# Purrfect Poetry

Lost Tower Publications asserts its copyright over this book as an anthology.

However, Lost Tower Publications does not have copyright for the individual poems printed herein.

Each contributor has kindly agreed to have their work published by Lost Tower Publications within this anthology.

The copyright of any of the poems published within remains the copyright of the authors.

The copyright of any of the photographs published within remains the copyright of the photographers.

Lost Tower Publications are a small, independent publishers.

Our aim is to recognise and showcase exciting new talents in the world of poetry.

©2014 by Lost Tower Publications

For further information please visit:
http://losttowerpublications.jigsy.com

# Purrfect Poetry

# Contents

# PURRFECT POETRY

Surprise

# PURRFECT POETRY

# Purrfect Poetry

# PURRFECT POETRY

## Jeanne Allen
# Smarty Cat

With caution stirs
Her sound she purrs
White stretched paws
Presents her claws
Buzz, a sound hassles
Her nose
One flying pest commands,
Controls
A moment for the puss, the cat
She is impulsive whacks one swat
The puss assured with what she got
The flee, a pest is now a dot

...Concerning Cats from the USA

## Linda Atterton
# The Butterfly Bush

A waterfall of honey filigree,
The butterfly tree is stars of violet blue,
A wizard's spell, ballet of snow set free,
A clumsy giant, my footsteps follow you,
A samba sway of cream in summertime,
An elfin child of moonlight come to play,
A somersault of limbs in pantomime,
A candlelight that danced to melt away.
The silhouette behind the windowpane,
The carousel of laughter set to rhyme,
The pirouette of seasons blurred her fall,
As one by one the steps fell out of time.
His paws an echo, silence fills my hall,
No plea will turn the tide of wintertime,
The labyrinth of feelings known as love,
The fragile song inside a velvet glove.

...of Cats from England

Linda Atterton
# The Tourmaline Cat

Two pointed ears like topiary covered in snow
To blue tourmaline eyes stare straight at you
Four paws dipped in finest milk chocolate
A nose like a shiny moist date

Bewitching rather than stalking
Parading not walking
A white Mercedes who purrs if you can afford him
Speeding through red lights if you try to ignore him

You don't buy him you make an investment
You can't own him you are the pet
Master of chaos who does not say please
Other cats are easy, he's Siamese

...of Cats from England

## Laura Beaudin
# Meow, Meow, Meow

Meow, Meow, Meow
Wake up you lazy human.
Meow
You hold me captive here so you must feed me. Now!
Meow
You are missing the best part of the day
Meow, Meow
Get up now!
That's right, now you are listening to me
Merp
Not that one, I want the other one.
When will you learn?
Meow
Finally!
You are dismissed now.

...of Cats from Canada

## Frances Blight
# Cat Boss

My pretty tortoiseshell cat so sleek and lean,
Lies under the bush so lush and green.
She sleeps silently and stays out all night,
Then wakes up and hunts purposefully all night.
A plucked bird, a soft vole or a chewed mouse,
Are often brought proudly into the house.
All the best vitamins and minerals are in her food,
But it's left there all day if she's not in the mood.
Sometimes she walks delicately along edges,
In front of the television or on ledges.
We can't see the picture but she is seen,
Precisely placing her paws so softly serene.
Tail aloft and with plenty of grace,
I'm the boss says the smile on her face.
She's here to stay with admiration and no danger,
That anyone here would ever change her.

...Concerning Cats from England

## Missy Buchanan
# The Cat in the Tuxedo

Yes? Yes? You call my name like I'm not listening. I am
listening. I just don't care. Oh. Wait. I hear the cold
cupboard door opening. Are you getting my milk?
What, woman? I'm already waiting beside my bowl.
What is it you want? Oh. You've stopped calling my
name. Now you're calling my Fatty Poo Pants like it's
cute. Like it's somehow better than my name. WHAT??
What is it you want? Yes. Just pour the milk into the
bowl and nobody gets hurt. Nobody has to lose an
eye here. Alright. Alright. You get three pats. Three
strokes of my head. But no more. Understand? Don't
talk baby talk. I'm not a baby. I am five years old!
Count them. FIVE. Just walk away. Wait. I own you. I
love you.
Go away now. You bore me.

...of Cats from New Zealand

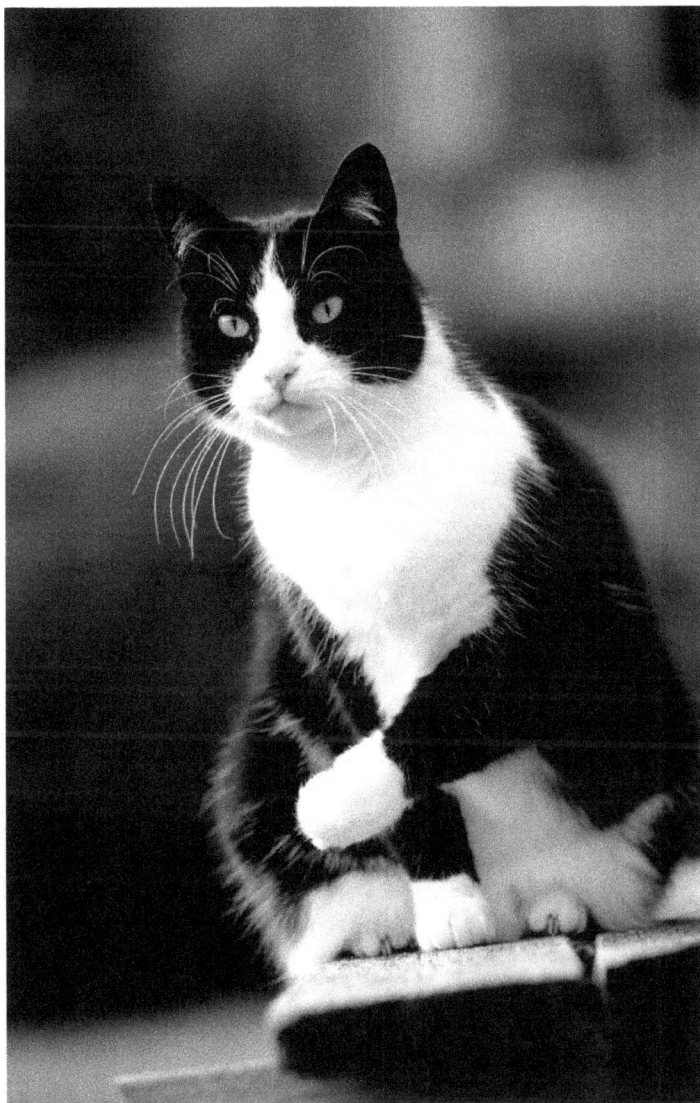

Cat in the Tuxedo

Lissie Bull
## Caught Napping....

Oh no.... you found me!
I thought I had the perfect spot
but sadly this was not to be
though I gave it my best shot

Its rather cosy here
please don't turf me out
all I wanted was to sleep
before I go and run about

Please let me nap awhile
as I'm cured up here to rest
you can have your bowl back soon
but right now, this is the best!!

...of Cats from England

Cat Napping

## Lissie Bull
## Feline Friends

Dirty foot prints across my work top
Neatly stacked papers knocked to the ground
A whisker lies there on the pillow
There has to be a cat somewhere around

Hear a jingling of a tiny bell
The soft meow from inside a box
Or a padding of paws across the boards
Purring as steady as the house clocks

Crashing of a vase that`s been knocked over
To the howling under the moon at night
Our feline friends are part of the family
Snuggled up asleep, so every thing`s alright

I am the servant for two wonderful cats!!

...of Cats from England

# Maryanne D. Brown Campbell
## Cat Haiku

Stalking creepily
Back arched, tail high, fur erect
Claws singe air and pounce

His purr my blanket
Pulled over my beating heart
The Mau Symphony

His entertainment
Am I, and my lap his bed
The cat owned human.

...Concerning Cats from the USA

## Adrian Ernesto Cepeda
# My Little Shadow

On my knee, with your orange tail
curling, Heaven knows I'm miserable
meow just like Morrissey sings;
I hear you coo like a restless chanteuse
but you don't need a microphone
to tell me you're already loathing
me distracted facing the computer screen.
Hate the sound of typing keys
signals less attention on you,
it must be Monday.
I feel your eyes blinking
softly asking: can you carry me
to that space between the ears
you love so much. Looking down,
my little shadow knows
I love the way
you slowly drift curling away
from cuddled kisses';
window whisk me, sniffing claws
scratching forever
living carpet diem dreams,
leave me sleepless, see you
snuggling the most adorable sounds
just to hear you snoring
licks upon my sockless
feet. My little shadow
I am weakened by your cuteness,
purring calmness awakens me
to your every scent
I find complete.

...Concerning Cats from the USA

Grey Cat Playing

## Wanda Morrow Clevenger
# Grey

a spatter grey
out the north field
trekked far
to my back door
handout
won't be shooed

desire for owning
furore best lent to
faithful
timmys and lassies

so many artful habitats
donated to auction,
birdcage last to go
- hardest to let go

and I am leery of this
grey under my porch
he makes himself
too much at home

...Concerning Cats from USA

## Drew Davis
# Drat That Cat
(A requiem)

No longer will the hairballs break
the stillness of the night
nor scratching on the bedpost
long before the morning light.

Her hungry, howling screeches
will not shatter afternoons,
nor mad careening dashes
scatter objects through the room.

I'm free from all her antics
that have plagued me from the start
except the diabolic way
she crept inside my heart.

...Concerning Cats from the USA

## Amitabh Vikram Dwivedi
# Beloved Cat

O my dear cat! My sweetheart!
You remind me of my love.
When you are near me, I am never alone.
You scratch me with your sharp claws.
It's your way to show love; there is no flaw.
Your dark cerulean eyes like some wild sea
Where I try to fathom out every mystery.
When I stroke your back; I forsake whatever I lack.
I lose my pain, my worries, and get pleasure
When I touch your agile body for good measure.
You are always near me as if you're my heart.
You are only my cat yet more lovable than my sweetheart.

...Concerning Cats from India

The Independent Tortoiseshell

## Omar Mohamed Eldamsheety
# Our Precious Cat

Some years ago
When I was a child
We lived in a small strange village
No cats existed in it.
Cats were living in all villages around it
But in that village
No cats at all
Why?
No one know
Dogs and rats,
but no cats
What should we do?
Rats were everywhere
free and happy
eating or just playing,
always they made troubles
Who will save us?
we asked hopefully
We need a cat
Only a cat can save us
A friend of my father
gave us his precious cat
mixed coloured, white and orange
How beautiful it was!
A lovely male cat
It lived with us
It believed that
It was one of the family
Slept in our bed
Ate our food
And played with us
as a brother,
not as our cat
We were so happy

But happiness is often short
We had to travel for two weeks
We couldn't take him with us
With our neighbours we left him
after they promised to take care
of our precious lovely cat
When we returned to the village
with too much longing
we asked about him
simply they answered
sorry, it died
with too much sadness and pain
How?
we asked,
It refused to eat cat food
and refused to sleep on the ground
it went out of the house
and we found it dead
they answered.
Oh My God,
We searched for it
We found its body
beside a dead rat
With our love we buried him
Goodbye our saviour
Goodbye our precious.

...of Cats from the Egypt

## Margaret Foster
# Russian Blue

Rescue haven, a stray little cat
front leg mangled, fur all matt.
No fluffy toy, this poor wee mite
eyes full of trust, denying his plight.

Minus his leg, fur closely shorn,
cuddled in blanket, cosy and warm.
Petted, pampered, he thrived and grew
soft velvet fur. A Russian Blue.

He rules the roost, this regal cat,
his lair my bed, kingdom my flat.
Beautiful beast so much adored,
faith in this world, renewed, restored.

Fills up my life with sparkle bright,
just being near holds true delight.
My shadow now this ball of fluff,
his trusting eyes, reward enough.

...of Cats from Australia

## Tim Graves
# Cat Haiku...

Shampooing my cat
Like juggling piranha fish
In a tsunami

...of Cats from England

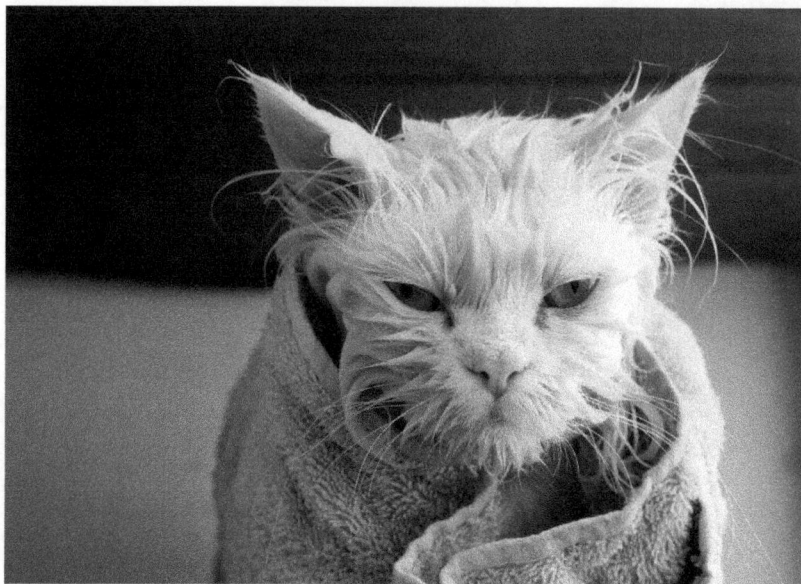

The Happiness of a Wet Cat

Ray Greenblatt
# Cat Sleeping

Cat is asleep for the long haul
completely unconscious
sinking into her pine needle nest
deeper and deeper
until she resembles
a piece of leftover
winter debris or
a stray dark plastic bag
which has snagged after
many a yard-blown trek.
With her variegated stripes and
Patches of grey, eggshell, tan
so soft in noon shine
she will wake only
to a sharp noise
a sharp scent
rouse then continue
her sentient life
never quite the same as
when I first beheld her.

...Concerning Cats from the USA

## Andrew W. Hale
# Cat Chili Floor Surprise

To my horror,
I
Had
Almost
Stepped
In
It.
Chili- brown. Unnatural.
Liquid. Chunks.
I started. Disbelief.
'Retch'
What end? Had it come out of....?
Coughing. Unsure. Afraid.
Scooper + Paper Towels=
Meagre. Weapons.
Smell. Unimaginable.
Closer. Gagging. Further.
Held breath.
Tears.
I scooped.

...Concerning Cats from the USA

# Rachael Z. Ikins
## Fear of Flying

12 years ago almost-birthday.
Muggy July, heat embargo.
10 p.m. My thighs stuck to vinyl.
Diesel fragrant air, tired tourists,
rumpled in, jackets lumped on arms,
meandering toward Baggage Claim.
I watched them dwindle.

All my losses, deaths, griefs- accumulated
weighted my ribs, my own stained satchel.
Corridors echoed, tourists vanished,
hydraulic doors hissed at the night
like a frightened cat.

My thighs stuck to vinyl.
Does the airport stay open 24/7?
At "too late" a blue-suited man entered
a secret door from the tarmac.

He carried my sharded heart,
white basket hung from one finger.
My thighs stung unstuck,
he smiled,
"Is this yours?"

I took my beating heart,
your carrier, my own two hands,
pressed my face, painful metal.
Blue crocheted baby-blanket inside.
two enormous ear-tips poking through.

This exact moment
I knew your wings;
that you had grabbed me
by my scruff,
would carry me high,
heal me of

my fear of flying
no matter how I squall.

...Concerning Cats from the USA

# Rachael Z. Ikins
## For Kate

Your hair smells like gin.
Crisp, of-the-forest, cold.
You spent a day hoarding
sunlight, posing on one
windowsill after another.
Washing yourself of winter.
You followed the light
east to west. By evening
you'd soaked so many
rays, you were gravid
with heat, gold, and
that juniper
scent. You hold my wrist
between your teeth, your
pupils dark moons, your sky-
blue eyes. You do not break
skin. I push my face into
your flank. I cannot resist you.
You murmur, a one-syllable
seduction. Throw yourself
onto/into weave, stories,
oriental rug. Bare pink,
pink belly to night's
rain-spangled
kiss.

...Concerning Cats from the USA

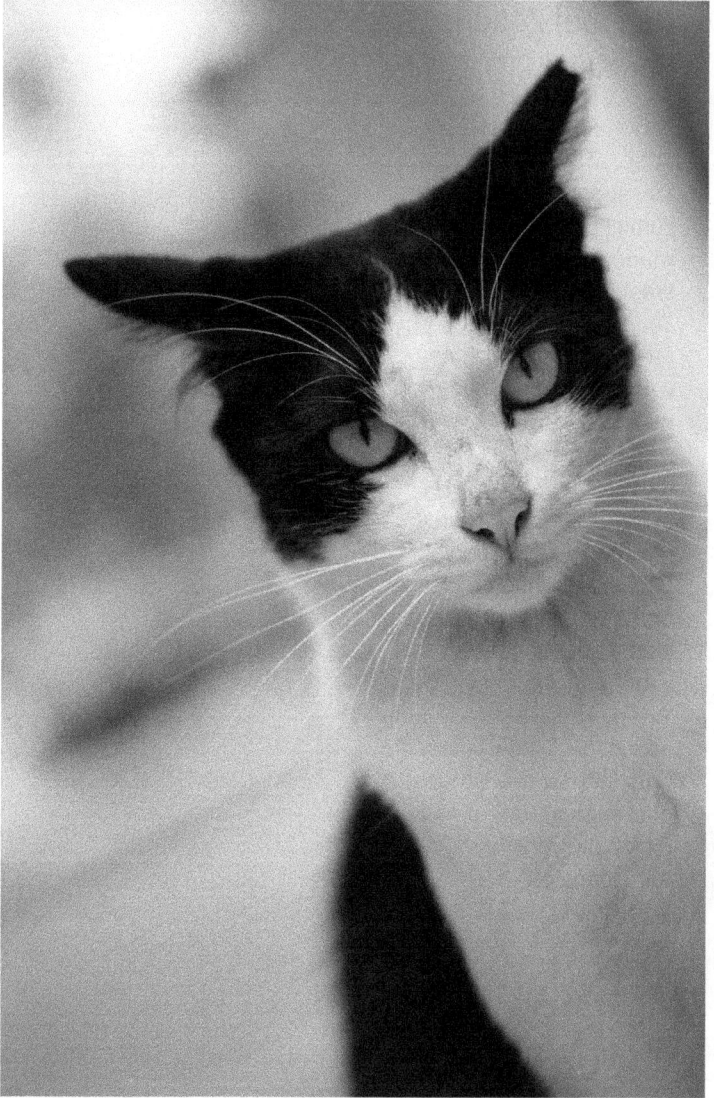

Bird Watching

Christina Johnson
# Playing With Cats

The female cat rolls over
On her back, looks up at
Me and begs. This time for
Her ball, which I toss down
The stairs and which she
Follows with a clatter and
A thump. At the bottom of
The stairs she looks up
At me as if to say, it's
Your turn. So I clatter
Down the stairs after her
And toss up the ball,
Which she follows with
Her eyes but no other part
Of her anatomy. This is
A bit of a one-sided game,
Where I throw the ball and
The cat chooses whether
To follow or to stay.

...Concerning Cats from the USA

# Debbie Johnson
## A Collection of Very Short Poems

as a brave mouse
runs across the kitchen floor
my 'cat-r-acts'


Cats
Chase mice
Until catch
Fresh rodent meat
Yum...


Mouse and me
Kitty makes three
Chases mouse
Around the house
A loud squeal
Cat satisfied
Mouse never heard from again


Cat bats paw in air
annoying fly buzzes by
feline fly swatter


Beautiful bright day
Cat on porch sunning herself
Feline tanning bed


black feline
stalks blue jay
seeking a supper
of fresh meat
on the fly

...Concerning Cats from the USA

Suzanne Kamata
# He's More of a Dog Person

Get off the table!
he shouts and Cat leaps
escaping his swat
slinks against the wall
in a feline sulk until
the wild takes over and he's
tearing down the hall
back and forth
pausing
only to rake the wallpaper
with claws,
Good for nothing bag of flees!
Cat flashes past
hides under a bed
creeps out to vomit
on the brand-new carpet
Okay, that's it. Back to the
street where we found you!
Finally, exhausted, Cat curls up
in a box
sleeps for hours until
he scoops up the ball of fur
cradles him, kisses cat gently
On the nose.
Who's your Daddy?

...of Cats from Japan

Daniel Klawitter
# What All Cats Know

Dogs are prose, and prone to please.
Mice are good for eating.
When moonlight splinters through the trees,
We watch humans while they're sleeping.
Disobedience is heroic.
It's wrong to persecute witches.
Hell is a world with no poets...
And heaven a charm of finches.

...Concerning Cats from the USA

The Bengal

## Erica Loberg
# Go Fetch

He likes to collect
Beer caps
Probably because he likes beer
And plays ice hockey with them
Across
The floor.

His latest me me me me now now now
Is to play go fetch
At 4 o'clock
In the morning.

He brings a cap
In his teeth
Jumps on my bed
While I am sleeping
And drops it

On my face.

Or he slides it
Under my hand
And head butts me
Waiting anxiously for me
To wake up
And throw it.

Eventually I give up
And toss it across the room
And watch him fly
Off the bed
To retrieve it.

And this goes on and off till
6 am
Two fun filled hours of morning "exercise"
If I don't play he cries...terrrrrible.

## Albert de Lorenzo
# Cat Poems

I never intended to be a poet.
Many will cheerfully say
I succeeded in that intent.
Yet I continue to write despite.

At moments like this, my brain
strains to come up with anything.
Writer's block has been hovering
for the better part of a week.

I feel like an empty vessel.
As my head droops,
I feel the primal soup
of my thoughts sloshing.

Slowly swinging my head
side to side like a confused bull
in a red bandanna shop,
sentence fragments drip,

drip, drop, drool onto the page
only to be wiped away,
brushed aside,
crumpled into paper balls.


The cats love them, these
crumpled paper poems,
they bat them about,
meowing for more.

Albert de Lorenzo

...of Cats from England

Cat in a Box

## Michelle Maciejewicz
# Friskie

Furry little buddy
Resting in the sky
Irreplaceable companion
Someone tell me why
Knowing how much I miss you
I still can't say goodbye
Eternity loving you, till the day I die.

...Concerning Cats from the USA

Sheila Marlin
# Mr Purrfect

My male cat
is hardly that.
Slim and sleek,
with dainty feet
and a jaunty walk,
his hind legs swagger
just like Mick Jagger's.
Flaunting elegant grace,
lifting a small, pointed face,
he portrays his disdainful air
with his neat, haughty stance.
No wonder that, at first glance,
these feline traits look, perchance,
as if Mr Purrfect should be Ms Kitty.
What a Wuss!

A scaredy cat,
he runs away at
any noise, any man,
the family, and even gran.
He retreats under the table,
from where he is safe and able
to lick himself, a constant habit.
He won't sit on chairs or my lap. It
is one unfriendly cat who just sleeps
all day, till he's hungry and then he creeps
around my legs, purring loudly in anticipation.
He will only have fish in jelly, meat he will not eat.
No trouble putting him to bed as he gets a tasty treat.
At night, he's a stop-out and hunts mainly mice, bringing
the remains of his prey for me, to discover in the morning.
So why do I keep him? He likes to be near me and I have
grown            .
fond of his constant company and his funny ways which has
shown
me that this decorative, pure white, graceful creature really
owns me!

What a Puss!

...of Cats from the England

Ian Mole
## The Cat
(with thanks to Ogden Nash)

The cat, I think we're all agreed,
will deal with mice if there's a need
and in addition to this boon
can soothe our tensions very soon.

...of Cats from England

Ian Mole
# Walking With the Harbour Cats

Hungry furry snakes
are gliding on all sides.
At every step
their number multiplies.
With heads and tails they're dancing
a feline pas-de-deux.
Petite Nijinskys camouflaged in fur.
A sinuous militia.
A padding palisade.
The Viet Cong shadows welcome their parade.

...of Cats from England

Jack Peachum
**Snapshot**
(Tigger)

Guessing my gloom, the old orange cat,
the warm smell of him –
arthritic, blind in one eye,
bitten by flea-devils,
he curls up beside me,
head-butting my arm for attention.
We are two elderly people
in a rainy afternoon.

...Concerning Cats from the USA

The Look of Love

# Winston Plowes
## Two Cats

My cats groom themselves
Vain contortionist coiffeurs
Lick fur... Content purr

Both my cats hunt mice
Miniature jungle tigers
Keep still... Torture, kill

My cats sleep all day
Long symmetrical slumbers
Squashed tail... piercing wail

Both my cats climb trees
Lofty feline ascenders
Scots Pine... 999

My cats play with string
Junior Gladiators
Too fast... Elastoplast

Both my cats eat grass
In creep regurgitators
Retch, yowl... kitchen towel

My cats have been ill
White coat investigators
Nothing found... £100

...of Cats from England

# Reena Prasad
## Purrspectives

Today we sat in perfect peace,
I on my easy chair
He on the window sill
Looking out together into the wintery garden
over the pebbles, at the fallen leaves
the burst of marigold sunshine, the guava laden trees
He stares gravely as if contemplating, perfectly still.
I watch his handsome face, wondering what he sees

His eyes give nothing away,
He seems to be smelling the breeze
while watching a butterfly
floating over the lawns at ease
I turn my chair toward him, to secretly read his thoughts.
Cleverer, he turns away as if to foil my plot
Does he wonder about the sun as it plays hide and seek
or accepts it without doubt as part of nature's decrees?

Maybe he wonders if I am out of my mind
sitting indoors though the weather is fine.
He bears with my every flaw, ever benign.
never going far, though I am rude sometimes
Do I live with him or does he live with me
An austere face, that stately walk- no less than any prince
Dignified and calm, his feline charm,
always soothes my hurt
A twitch of his tail, his ears go up, he crouches down, alert!

He sees a bird, I know
his inborn instincts keeping time
One of us is a poet-which one?
but together, our days do rhyme

...Regarding Cats from India

It's Always the Quiet Ones

## P.J.Reed
# Scoring Highly on the Psychopathy Scale

I am worried about the
Career aspirations of my cat;
The nightly stalking and the
Dismemberments on our mat.

She distains from human contact
Ignores commands to sit or stay;
In quest for isolation
Sleeping in her box all day.

Loving me in purring tones
Seducing every dinner time;
Compulsive public licking
Hides the evidence of her crime.

Sated; flicks her tail and leaves
To that dark world beyond my door;
While I wait in nightly fear
Of bodies on my kitchen floor.

...of Cats from England

A Family Portrait

# Elisavietta Ritchie
## Soft Spots, for a Deaf Siamese Cat

She, a skinny princess fallen on hard times.
I heard her purrs. She could not, nor our
learned conversations above her head. She—

> Siamese, like the destitute prince my
> father rescued in a blizzard, student
> searching for a flop house in an odd
> district in Chicago.  Sent to study in
> America, his funds soon ran out. My
> father brought him home to a couch
> shared with our angora tabby, King
> Tutankhamen, who warmed him all
> Christmas week—(I kept that couch
> years,  for other strangers and cats).

Today, my hosts pushed her off her chair so
I could sit down though I demurred. This act
required my offer of lap and a good caressing.

> In Greek the word for stranger and guest
> the same: *ksenos*. Did my Russian émigré
> father tell his stranger/guest how once he
> trudged snowy battlefields seeking safety,
> reached Ellis Island penniless midwinter,
> slogged through storms on a New Haven
> campus, shovelled coal, tutored calculus,
> French, to pay for meals, books, clothes?
> My father was merely related to princes.

I warmed her elderly feline bones, did not
murmur baby talk she could not hear,  or
mind she left beige hairs  on black slacks.

> Fifty year passed. My father's job took him
> to Bangkok. The prince, doing well, greeted
> him warmly. Both preferred tropical climes,
> kept cats, shared incipient hearing problems.

My hosts offered to rent me their deaf
Siamese cat. I will take her at any time
and I too rescue strays in a blizzard...

...Concerning Cats from the USA

## Belinda Rogers
# The New Cats

scratching at my canvas
pulling at my cloth
this little ball of chaos
running here and there

my brushes on the floor
coffee on my notes
the gravity of solitude
loosening from my grasp

vertigo in hidden places
peeing on the rug
a perilous pique
calling for my hand

pulling at my senses
tugging on my sock
something in the studio

falling

a noise within the darkness
a tiny little purr
in my silence it is said
the silent thing is waiting

...of Cats from New Zealand

A Family Dinner

Sarah Russell
# Cat Nap

The cat invited me to fill my lap
with heavy, lithe contentment.
We curled together on the couch,
purring pressure
as she arched her neck against my hand,
languid comfort,
her body nestled into mine.

I roused,
my hand still stroking lightly
in my sleep,
cat vanished to other ventures,
the niche indented by her form
still vibrant with her warmth,
fingertips caressing air
in silken touch remembrance.

...Concerning Cats from the USA

# Ibrahim Ibn Salma
## Boosy the Cat

Paws of grey and white,
Softly pawing on my side,
Sounding;
Meow Meow Meow,
I hear;
Love Love Love.
When love is wordless,
Love is vast.

...Concerning Cats from the USA

Don Schaeffer
## Wanting a Rub

When the cat
jumps on the bed
she wants her rub.
Millions of packets
of animal expectation
pass between us.

Rub just above her eyes,
pushing her flickery ears
back and forth.
Rub between her shoulder blades
hard and down behind her neck
over her collar bone.

When she arrives just as I'm getting up
I almost want to stay and rub her
to keep from breaking her tiny heart.
Although I will say cats stay alive
through many more disappointments
than people.

...Concerning Cats from the USA

## Aditya Shankar
# Meow, in chorus with My Cat

How I love the taste of words when
you say nothing.

Meow, it means fish,
It means boredom, pride.

You are the better lyric poet.
Meow, and you say everything-
condensed like ice, preserved
for a day of bad fortunes.

And you know our story is like an
Indian movie – starring,  you the cat
and me the tiger, Soon, you turn
tiger and I am the cat.

I hear the clatter of vessels from
the kitchen, the odour of milk.

At the clatter of kitchen vessels
the odour of milk.
I say nothing.

I'm the cat.
Sometimes, you are also a cat.
And It means, we're no more alone.

...Regarding Cats from India

# Sunil Sharma
## Child and Cat in a High-Rise

The cat lies curled up on the landing
Of the posh high-rise in Mumbai,
An intruder slipping in/out sans
Raising alarm among the residents or security,
So fleet-footed is the little feline, unseen by these;
A bundle of furs for the solitary child caged inside
A large house, looking out on the Arabian Sea,
Amid toys and plasma TV but no company;
The cat and the girl-child exchange looks,
She pats the new visitor smuggled inside
By her conspiring maid, not terrified
Of the cats, coming from a village
Where humans and cats live side-by-side,
And the girl gets a purring friend that meows
At the touch of the docile child,
And spreads cheers among two lonely lives.

...Regarding Cats from India

Walking on the Wild Side

## Carol A. Stephen
# Small Attentions

a small device voices alarm,
humming its unfamiliar tune
to Cat, who stops in his kitty-paw path
along desktop, eyes fixed
upon this curiosity. His gaze
is steady, but his eyes move,
a small motion, not quiver but shiver,
a shimmer so swift, almost invisible,
his small attention a deep
and thorough meditation
before his body loses tension,
relaxes into his usual pose
of inward-facing cat.

...of Cats from Canada

## Patricia Feinberg Stoner
# The Tyranny of Cats

The sun of southern France beat down
And forced us to retreat
To stone-flagged kitchen. Sipping wine
We cowered from the heat.

Then suddenly my husband said
"Look! There's a cat in here."
And I replied, as wives reply,
Indulgently: "Yes, dear."

Had he. I wondered, drunk too deep?
The wine was strong, I knew.
Or had he simply nodded off
And dreamed? But it was true:

To catch the slightest breath of air
The kitchen door stood wide;
The cat had seen a welcome there
And slipped unseen inside.

It stood and mewed, as cats will mew,
And with imperious stance
It clearly said "Now give me milk."
And thus began the dance.

For such a merry dance he led
Us, all that summer through
He'd but to voice a whim and we
Obeyed, as humans do.

At crack of dawn he would appear
And yowl until we rose.
We gave him milk, we gave him fish
And cuddles- when he chose.

But summer passed as summers will
And it came time to leave.

"What will become of him?" I sobbed.
There was no need to grieve.

When he saw suitcases come out
(He knew what they were for)
Without a backwards glance he left
And found a bed next door.

For cats are independent folk
They don't need us, and that's
The underlying secret of
The tyranny of cats.

...of Cats from England

Taking a Stroll

## Karen Stromberg
## The Third Cat

Half Siamese, half celebrity
your eyes are full of pale sky
and your chaotic history. Capote
of cats, whose witty claws widen
the periphery of your domain,
you distort the Shih Tzu's
personality. Anything new
and your nose is there. Wilde cat
I adore your earnest commentaries.
Houdini of felines, I love how
you disappear and reappear, twice
the size of what you are
in that flamboyant cloud of fur.

...Concerning Cats from the USA

S. Tarr
## A Man Can Dream

I saw a lovely girl today,
she played the cello,
she stared at me,
and that made me mellow.

I said to my cat,
my friend and fellow,
"A man can dream, boy,
a man can dream".

He, of course, did not,
say anything back,
because he is a cat,
and cats can't do that.

...Concerning Cats from South Africa

## Barbara Thomas
# Mrs. Watkins' One-Eyed Cat

Mrs. Watkins' one-eyed cat
Is tortoiseshell, and rather fat,
And whether it be sun or rain
From cushioned seat by window-pane,
With his remaining amber eye
He watches people passing by.
He does not care for catching mice
Or eating tuna mixed with rice.
His preference is fine white fish,
Served in his own blue china dish
A piece of tasty cod or hake,
For afters likes Madeira cake.
When nature's call can't be ignored
Or even when he's feeling bored
He will politely scratch the door
With one insistent snow-white paw
So Mrs. Watkins, quietly sitting
Will put aside her pale-pink knitting
To wander down the linoed hall
Past pictures hung on either wall
To let him out with warning words
Regarding never chasing birds.
A cat-flap she won't entertain
Afraid it will admit the rain
As well as other cats who could
Come prowling round the neighbourhood
To trespass on her Tom's domain
Or look out through his window-pane
For though he may be rather fat
Tom would not kindly take to that.
His turn of speed belies his size
When taking others by surprise.
But curled on Mrs. Watkins' lap
He's such a friendly, loving chap
There's really no denying that
Of Mrs. Watkins' one-eyed cat.

...of Cats from England

Cats and Boxes

Rachel Tobin
# Brinny

Sea laps light from the brimming sky;
the swerve of coastline slips off
her silver wrap, beneath the breast of Kapiti.
In the kitchen, you're poised to jump.

The swerve of coastline slips off her silver wrap:
a dream house leans out to watch.
In the kitchen, you're poised to jump;
a new-born cake cools on the designer bench.

A dream house leans out to watch;
the sea craves sky on coast.
The new-born cake on the bench
falls prey to your teeth and whisker.

The sea craves sky on coast.
My homecoming is clawed clunks
and crumbs, prey to teeth and whisker.
I cried good tears into that cake.

My homecoming is clawed chunks and crumbs
and you look sweeter than ever, Brinny boy.
I cried good tears into that cake,
free-range chocolate, organic eggs.

You look sweeter than ever, Brinny;
day by day you cat your way into my heart.
Full with free-range chocolate, organic eggs;
your milk-built ears twitch and dream.

Day by day you cat your way into my heart.
Silver wraps beneath the breast of Kapiti.
Your milk-built ears weave twitch and dream.
Sea laps light from the brimming sky.

# Jonathan Tromane
## Seduction

That look, those staring eyes.
I feel them upon me now,
Probing every part of my body.
A look of desire and adulation.
The smile, almost a smirk,
Confirming what she is seeking.
She wants me, all to herself.

I sit in my chair, tense.
Our eyes lock on each other.
My pulse rate quickens.
I uncross my legs in anticipation.
She moves slowly
Uncoiling herself for me.
A pink tongue and white teeth appear.
She licks her lips sensuously.
She interprets my smile as a yes.

She stands and stretches,
Her body lithe and athletic.
I am envious of her flexibility.
Her movements are so graceful
As she slowly bridges the gap.
I stretch my legs out,
Arms by my sides, my breathing shallow.
I am ready for her.

In a millisecond she is on my lap
I gasp waiting for her next move
I caress her neck
My fingers glide along her back
She is so beautiful.
She slowly settles upon me.
Her tail flicks my face

Then the purring starts.
She has me where she wants me,
Until it's time for her nightly feed.

...of Cats from Australia

British Grey Cat...

## Sylvia Riojas Vaughn
# Punkin Puss

I don't know where
Father got you.
Orange,
white stockings,
three months.
I rub my cheek
against your wiggling body.
I don't know why
Mother blushes at the vet
when they call your name.
Your rough tongue tickles –
purring, hypnotic.
When you hear the whirring
can opener, you race
to our sunny kitchen.
If we play checkers,
you leap aboard.
You climb the telephone pole
in our front yard, yowl
until rescue.
I'd like to know
if you dream
of fields and fields
of catnip.

...Concerning Cats from the USA

## Sally Zakariya
# Why We Live With Cats

Why we live with cats is a puzzle when it's dogs that care
that want to do our bidding, all waggy and breathy and jumpy
when we come in and cats all ho hum at the best of times

languorously licking and preening and keeping their secrets
behind those eyes that aren't yellow or green like the kids'
books
say but something unfathomably other.

Why we live with cats when the couch is clawed to fuzz
is anybody's guess, but personally I think it might
be a matter of reaching for the unattainable.

Stingy with affection, they give what they want
to give, when they want to give it, slitting those
aforementioned eyes, making that cats-only

comfortable rumble, smiling enigmatically.
We're instantly smitten and not just because we don't
have to walk them or pick up their mess

not because they police the rodents, which was useful
back when we all had our own granaries but less
of a plus in these domestically manicured days

and certainly not because like dogs they love us
lavishly but because—silly humans that we are—we keep
thinking we can earn their singular regard.

by Sally Zakariya

...Concerning Cats from the USA

# Cigeng Zhang
## A Civet Cat

A baby civet cat
Black and grey haired
Bathed a cold shower
in the midnight rain
Ran out aimlessly
Lost her way
She cried
miao-miao, sounded
Like a little doll.

I just walked
in the morning street
My shoes, red shoes
Ceased her cry
She stopped at my feet
Looked up at my face
Big eyes like black currants
Little claws tried
to grasp my long skirt

Begging for food
I understood
Darling, wait, wait
I searched my bag
Quickly
A piece of chocolate found
I leaned over
Fed the little cat
She ate in haste
miao miao she called
as if calling "mama"

I am sorry little cat
Nothing more left in my bag

## PURRFECT POETRY

If I was not in an alien place
I'd have taken you home
Crossing over the vast sea
To our home to find you a dad.

...Concerning Cats from the China

# Biography of Poets

# Biography of Poets

**Linda Atterton** has published poetry in a number of magazines including *The Moth*, *Abridged*, and *Litro*. She has just finished her first novel, set in Norfolk. She works with people affected by head injuries.

**Laura Beaudin** is new to poetry but is very familiar with cats. She is currently owned by Mickey and Honey.

**Frances Blight** is an English Literature graduate and was a teacher for many years. She has written all her life and has been published in many anthologies. She is particularly inspired by her family and the beautiful Devon countryside.

**Missy Buchanan** has a Bachelor of Arts in English Literature and one-third of a Bachelor of applied Arts in Creative Writing. She works in a cubicle. Missy Buchanan lives in New Zealand.

**Lissie Bull** is from Bristol. She is a widow and mother of four who took up writing in 2007. Lissie loves expressing emotions in verse and painting pictures through the use of words. She has had her poems included in a few anthologies and there are over 900 poems on her blog:
http://lissiebullpoetry.blogspot.co.uk

**Maryanne D. Brown Campbell** is author of the books *Serpentine Tongue* and *Food for the Soul*. These books are available at Barnes & Nobles, Amazon and Author House.

**Adrian Ernesto Cepeda** is an L.A. poet whose work appears in the new *True Romance Poems* collection, *1000 Tankas for Michael Brown*, *The Lake Poetry*, *Edgar Allen Poet Journal # 2*, *Fukushima Poetry Anthology*, *San Gabriel Valley Poetry Quarterly*, *Spilt Ink Poetry*, *Luna Luna Magazine's Latino*

*Poetry Project, Love Poetry Lovers, The Rain, Party, & Disaster Society* and in the soon to be released, *Men's Heartbreak Anthology* and Poetry. He is currently enrolled in the MFA Graduate program at Antioch University in Los Angeles.

**Wanda Morrow Clevenger** lives in Hettick, Il, Over 287 pieces of her work appear in 110 print and electronic publications. This is her only poem written about a cat. Visit her magazine blog at: **http://wlc-wlcblog.blogspot.co.uk**

**Drew Davis** is a poet, playwright and author near Augusta, Georgia USA. More of his work can be found at:
www.drew-davis.com

**Amitabh Vikram Dwivedi**, a linguist by profession, has been working as an assistant professor in the School of Languages and Literature at Shri Mata Vaishno Devi University, Katra, India. His recent publications, *A Linguistic Grammar of Hadoti* (2012) and *A Grammar of Bhadarwahi* (2013) by Lincom Europa Academic Publications (Germany) and a register of the lesser known Indo-Aryan languages in India. As a poet, his fifty poems have made place in various anthologies worldwide. Recently, his poem 'Mother' has been included as a prologue to *Motherhood and War: International Perspectives* (2014) by Palgrave Macmillan Press.

**Omar Mohamed Eldamsheety** is an Egyptian poet. He was born in 21/08/1978 in Tanta, Egypt. Omar has been writing Arabic poetry since 1989. He started writing poetry in English in 2014.

**Ray Greenblatt's** new eBook—*Twenty Years on Graysheep Bay*—is now available.

**Andrew Hale** is currently a graduate student at Our Lady of The

Lake University. A native of Texas, Andrew does not enjoy excessive heat or cold.

**Rachael Ikins** is a prize winning poet and artist who began to write about her cats when she was 7 years old. She continues to find her muse in feline eyes and shares her home with Kate and two dachshunds.

**Debbie Johnson** began writing poetry 4 years ago as a therapeutic way of coping with being disabled. She has written two books; *The Disability Experience* and *The Disability Experience II.*

**Suzanne Kamata** is an American living in Japan. She is the author of three novels, including *Screaming Divas.* She teaches EFL and Creative Writing at the University of Tokushima.

**Daniel Klawitter** is a widely published poet and member of the Colorado Poets Center. He has 4 cats and is the lead singer/lyricist for the indie folk-rock band, *Mining for Rain.*

**Erica Loberg** has a Tabby cat named *The Fat Man*. He lives a comfortable life in a loft in Downtown Los Angeles. He's there for Erica through tough times and they share the best of times together too. Without him, she'd be someone else.

**Albert de Lorenzo** is the author of two books: *Of Aging Angst* and *Taken Aback in Passing.* His books are available in print from http://stores.lulu.com/oddbrainpress
His books are also available for immediate sampling and sale in multiple eBook formats, readable on virtually any eBook reading device. For further information please visit his website at http://www.oddbrainenterprises.com

For **Michelle Maciejewicz** creative writing and poetry is a passion, the hearts way of expressing true emotions.

**Sheila Marlin** is an artist and writer. She has written two books. She is the co-author of *A Grandparent's Survival Guide to Childcare* and author of *Flip to the Rescue*.

**Ian Mole** is from Sunderland but has lived in London for many years. He is a Teacher of English to overseas students and is a Rock and Roll Tour Guide in London.

**Jack Peachum** is a contemporary poet who draws his inspiration from many different sources. This poem is a 'Gatha', an ancient Chinese eight line poem.

Living on a boat on a canal in West Yorkshire, England **Winston Plowes** spends his days learning poetry from his lucky black cat, 'Fatty' who says that after many years he is finally showing some promise.

**Reena Prasad** is a poet from India, now based in Sharjah. She has poems published in the online journals: *Carty's Poetry Journal*, *Indian Ruminations*, *Indian Review*, *Angle Journal*, *The Copperfield Review*, *First Literary Review-East*, *The Indian River Review* and in books by Poetry quarterly, Lost Tower Publications, Brian Wrixon and Barry Mowles etc.

**P.J.Reed** is an author, poet and sometime photographer. She specializes in speculative fiction, writing mainly Dark Romantic and Gothic Horror poetry. Her work has featured in many anthologies and essay writing guides. Her first collection of work entitled *The Wicked Come* and is available from Amazon and all good bookshops. Her Gothic Horror Literature site is found at: http://thewickedcome.com

**Elisavietta Ritchie** has had her poems, fiction, articles, widely published, anthologized and translated. She has published

sixteen poetry collections, recently *Tiger Upstairs on Connecticut Avenue*; *Feathers, Or, Love on the Wing*; *Cormorant Beyond the Compost*, *Tightening The Circle Over Eel Country* won the Great Lakes Colleges Association's "New Writer's Award." Her fiction includes *Flying Time*; *In Haste I Write You This Note.* She is the Washington Writers' Publishing House ex-president poetry and ex-president fiction. Her work can be found at: **www.elisaviettaandclyde.com**
Painter and Poet **Belinda Rogers** work can be found at: www.thedreamingseed.com

You can see more of **Sarah Russell's** work by visiting her website at: http://www.sarahrussellpoetry.com

**Ibrahim Ibn Salma** is a poet and a spiritual scientist. He has been inspired by nature and her soul, by a world whose purpose of existence is to be most loving and by his affinity with his growth as a spiritual being, which he takes very seriously. *Traveller* and *House of Love* are his first two collections of poems. "Who created the universe and why?" is his first parable with poetic flavour.

**Don Schaeffer** is a retired social scientist and amateur poet. He is also a ghost blog writer.

**Aditya Shankar** writes and publishes poetry, flash fiction and he has had articles published in leading internal journals. He is the author of two books of poems, with the latest being *Party Poopers* (2014). Aditya completed his B.tech from CUSAT, Cochin and currently lives and works in Bangalore, He is passionate about gamification and social contents and works on the same at Innovatia, India. His website is found at: **http://adityashankar.tumblr.com**

Mumbai-based, **Sunil Sharma,** a college principal, is also a

widely-published bilingual Indian critic, poet,
literary interviewer, editor, translator, essayist and fiction
writer. His six short stories and the novel *Minotaur* were
recently prescribed for the undergraduate classes under the
Post-colonial Studies, Clayton University, USA. He is
the recipient of the UK-based Destiny Poets' inaugural poet of
the year for 2012.

**Carol A. Stephen** has had poetry published in several Ontario
journals, anthologies and online at TLE
http://thelightekphrastic.com. She won third place in the
Canadian Authors National Capital Writing Contest 2012. Her
chapbooks are: *Above the Hum of Yellow Jackets* and
*Architectural Variations*. Her work is found at:
http://quillfyre.wordpress.com

**Patricia Feinberg Stoner** loves dogs, cats and some people.
She lives in beautiful West Sussex with her husband, also a
writer, and a mad spaniel. She is the author of *Paw Prints in
the Butter* a collection of humorous cat verses. You can find
out more at:
https://www.facebook.com/pages/Paw-Prints-in-the-
Butter/719210834795177?fref=ts

**Karen Stromberg** is a poet and flash fiction writer. She, and
her husband, have three rescue cats, an ancient Shih Tzu, and
Tony, the Siamese.
**S. Tarr** is a writer of poems, stories and other daring thoughts.
Discover more at: **http://chronicles.co.za**

**Barbara Thomas** lives in a large mobile home in West
Cornwall. As well as poetry she also writes epic fantasy and
her first novel, as B J Beach is released in November 2014.

**Rachel Tobin** has lived in New Zealand since she was nine; her
ancestors lived in Ireland, England and France. She lives on

the lovely Kapiti Coast north of Wellington and her first collection of poetry is in the process of publication. Rachel writes because of her deep enjoyment of words and their power to move, inspire and invite new ways of seeing.

**Jonathan Tromane** is a creative writer of poems, short stories & novels. For more information please see his website: **www.jonathant7.wix.com/jtcreative**

**Sylvia Riojas Vaughn's** work is pending in *Triadæ Magazine*, and has appeared in *Diálogo*, *Label Me Latina/o,* and *Desde Hong Kong: Poets in conversation with Octavio Paz.*

**Sally Zakariya** is a life-long cat owner who lives and writes in Arlington, Virginia, USA. Her poetry has appeared in numerous journals and won prizes from Poetry Virginia and the Virginia Writers Club. She has published two chapbooks.

**Cigeng Zhang** is a freelance English translator from China. She has an English degree and began writing poems in English in April 2012.

# Photograph Credits

| | | |
|---|---|---|
| Cat | Photographed by Wineglas | Front |
| Black and White Cat | This cat in his tuxedo was photographed by Barbie. | 15 |
| Sleeping Kitten | Sleeping kitten playing with a ball of yarn was photographed by Lilun. | 16 |
| Grey Cat Playing | Dimitris Kolyris is a photographer from Greece. | 21 |
| The Tortoiseshell | P.J.Reed is a speculativce poet and writer from Devon, England. Her wwork is reknown for its dark, dramatic imagery and restrained use of language. One of her hobbies is black and white photography. Which can be seen on her website at: http://thewickedcome.com | 25 |
| Wet Cat | Wet Cat was photographed by Fotosmile. | 30 |
| Angry Cat | Angry Cat was photographed by Unteroffizier | 36 |
| Young Bengal Cat on Stairs | By photographer Steve Heap | 41 |
| Cat in a box | Photographed by Jinny Dion of Pointe-Lebel, Canada | 44 |
| Funny Garfield Cat | Dimitris Kolyris is a photographer from Greece | 51 |
| Cat Yawning | Photographed by Milena Bildova from the Czech Republic. | 54 |

# PURRFECT POETRY